YOUR

SITUATION

DOESN'T

DETERMINE

YOUR

DESTINATION

Joshua Watson

Gotham Books

30 N Gould St.
Ste. 20820, Sheridan, WY 82801
https://gothambooksinc.com/

Phone: 1 (307) 464-7800

Published by Gotham Books (July 19, 2024)

ISBN: 979-8-3302-9633-0 (P)
ISBN: 979-8-3302-9634-7 (E)

Table of Contents

Introduction

Life's like a book, full of different chapters, and mine's a tale of bouncing back, embracing change, and celebrating victories. I came into this world on August 12, 2003, amidst some rough times, with big things happening globally and plenty of personal struggles to boot. From family fights to figuring out the foster care system, my early years weren't exactly a walk in the park.

My arrival happened alongside some major world events, like the fallout from the Iraq War and political shake-ups in Liberia. As the sixth kid in the Crosby crew, born to Anita and Ronald Crosby, I grew up in a household where arguments were common, and money was often scarce.

But in the middle of all that chaos, there were moments of hope. My foster parents, Mary, and Edward Watson, took me in with open arms, giving me stability and love when I needed it most. Despite the challenges, they made sure I had a safe space to grow and figure things out.

My journey to figuring out who I am started early. With support from my foster family and some awesome teachers, I tackled problems head-on and learned a lot along the way.

Today, my story's all about bouncing back and holding onto hope. Even when things got tough, I managed to come out stronger on the other side. My journey's proof that with a bit of grit and determination, you can overcome pretty much anything.

As I keep moving forward, I'm taking the lessons I've learned with me. Fueled by resilience and kindness, my story's all about inspiring others to face life's ups and downs with courage and a positive attitude.

In the journey of life, we come across various individuals who leave an indelible mark on our path. Among them, Ms. June Gonzalez stands out as a significant influence. Her parting words, "Your Situation Doesn't Determine Your Destination," deeply resonate with me and have become the cornerstone of this book. Reflecting on her profound insight, I realize how it encapsulates the essence of my personal journey.

Ms. Gonzalez's words serve as a beacon of hope, reminding me that despite life's challenges, we possess the agency to shape our destiny. Each encounter, no matter how brief, contributes to the intricate tapestry of our experiences. Through her wisdom, I find comfort in the knowledge that adversity does not dictate our future. Instead, it is our resilience and determination that pave the way forward.

Reflecting on the intricate interplay between personal and global events, I find myself drawn to the remarkable resilience that emerged amidst the turmoil. As the world grappled with seismic shifts, our family's journey mirrored the ebb and flow of these larger forces. Yet, amid the chaos, there were moments of grace and strength, embodied by figures like my foster parents, who provided a steady anchor in the storm.

How can our personal journeys mirror the challenges and triumphs of the world around us? What sustains us through the trials of life, both on a personal and collective level? Can storytelling offer solace and strength in the face of adversity? These questions resonate deeply with the themes of resilience, hope, and the power of human connection that permeate this narrative.

Chapter 1

The day started on August 12, 2003, when the cost of milk was $2.76. Wow! Those were the good old days when things were inexpensive compared to what it is today. On that day, I was born at 2:45 pm to my parents, Anita, and Ronald Crosby, and named Joshua Tyler Crosby. My family at the time was divided due to my parents running away from home, and my siblings were later taken from our grandmother and raised in foster care.

Although I don't know much about my real family, I do know that my uncle had just gotten out of deployment from the war with Iraq in March of that year, when the US destroyed Iraq's weapons of mass destruction and ended Saddam Hussein's rule.

As stated by my uncle, "Being in the Iraq war was one of the scariest things in my life. I remembered being escorted on one of the biggest planes I had ever seen, the C130, where I had a team of 50–75 people on the flight. When I got to Iraq, it was pitch black. Once we got off the plane, we were given armor, guns, and ammo. After that, we were divided into groups and infiltrated camps and bases." (Brown, October 8th)

"On Wednesday, March 19, 2003, President George W. Bush ordered the invasion of Iraq. As he explained that night in an address to the nation, this military operation, known as Operation Iraqi Freedom, was to disarm Iraq, free its people, and

1

defend the world from grave danger. To accomplish these objectives, the United States and its coalition partners used military force to strike "selected targets of military importance to undermine Saddam Hussein's ability to wage war." (William C. Martel, 2006)

Also, on that day of my birth, Liberian President, Taylor, stepped down and went into exile in Nigeria. Four people, including two suicide bombers, died in the back-to-back attacks in Israel and the West Bank. President Bush had nominated Utah governor, Michael Leavitt, to head the Environmental Protection Agency, replacing Christie Todd Whitman who resigned in May. (Democracy Now, 2003)

I am the sixth child of the nine my mother had; out of my dad's twelve, I am number eight. My mom and dad were both low-income parents who could not afford the children they had. "They had been dating since high school," my adoptive mom told me. They had dropped out of school together and ran away from home to keep their relationship intact since their parents did not approve of them dating. When I was born, it was only my mom, dad, sister, and I because our four older siblings were taken away in foster care.

In 2005 and 2007, my younger brother and sister (Samuel and Aaliyah) were born, and my mom had two miscarriages in the years 2004 and 2006 (causes unknown). My dad was never the best husband or father, he would stay home and do whatever he wanted while my mom would go and help at a hair salon. We never had a home of our own, but we were given somewhere to live by the government until we had enough money to rent or buy a house somewhere.

My dad became abusive over time, and he was using all the money we got from the government to gamble all the time. He also bought himself video games. When it came to food, he wouldn't even try to get a proper meal for us to eat. Every week, we would go to a store to steal food since he didn't want to spend his gambling money.

Living in the Bronx wasn't easy at all during that time because of all the problems it had with police and violence. So, growing up in our apartment was absolutely the worst. We lived in a basement that was continuously infested with rats and roaches, and since it was a one-bedroom apartment, we all had to cram into that one bed to sleep. We would often end up going to bed hungry at night.

One day, at the age of three, my sister and I decided to go out and get food because we were starving. At that moment the only way we could get food was by going to the store, taking the food, hiding it in our pockets, and taking it home.

Since we were too short to open the house door at that time, we decided to break the window and climb out to go to the store. On our way to the store, we were found by the police. They took my sister and me in their car and gave us something to eat since we were very malnourished.

Then, they decided to take us home and noticed the broken window. Upon seeing how thin we were, they realized we were being neglected. So, they barged into the house, saw its condition, and examined my siblings and me.

We were taken to a hospital to be examined, where we were diagnosed with ADHD and ADD. Then, due to the neglect they witnessed, we were put into foster care.

Figure 1: "My little brother, sister, and I found ourselves nestled on the bed of our adopted parents."

Figure 2 : "My sibling, adopted father, and I relaxing together on the couch."

Chapter 2

Little Flower was founded by Monsignor Bernard J. Quinn in the year 1929 to help homeless kids that were either orphaned, abandoned, or neglected, to find good homes. They are a company that helps children around the five boroughs get the love and help they need. The first child they received was Walter Smith in the 1930s-1940s. (History)

In the early 2000s, they officially changed their name from Little Flower Children's Services of New York to Little Flower Children and Family Services of New York. They were awarded one of the largest contracts in NYC to serve Brooklyn youths at risk of out-of-home placement due to their involvement with the juvenile justice system as part of the Juvenile Justice Initiative (JJI). (History)

In the year 2000, they started the B2H program, otherwise known as Bridges to Health, where social workers were hired to visit children every week to evaluate how they are doing in their new homes and how the families were treating them. The workers gave the children different goals to help them overcome fears or traumas due to whatever happened to them in their past. (History)

Chapter 3

Mary Samuels and Edward Watson were born in the parish of Saint James, Montego Bay. Mary had five siblings and Edward had seven siblings. Mary came to America since her mom, Nella Samuels, was already in America, and she had the chance to migrate. Edward Watson came to America because he was accepted to do farm work in the states and due to his poor upbringing, he decided to take the job. (Mary, October 2022)

Mary Samuels and Edward Watson met at the Bank of America where Edward said it was love at first sight. According to Edward, "After that day, I would always go to the bank just to see if I would find her there again. One day, I prayed that we would run into each other again if she were the one. Luckily, we did, and after that, we started dating, and the rest is history. On the 12th of August 2000, we got married." (Edward, October 2022)

Mary and Edward had the desire to have kids but couldn't because of certain complications. During that time, they sat and discussed the decision to adopt since they had the space and wanted to impact someone's life. So, they decided to visit foster children to help them in any way they could.

So, the adoption agency they choose was Little Flower Agency and it was decided that my siblings and I were chosen to be adopted by Mary and Edward. After the incident with the police, my mom and dad (Anita Crosby and Ronald Crosby) were arrested due to the conditions we were in and how our home looked, which put us straight into foster care where my siblings and I were moved from the Bronx to Long Island.

Our new parents, Mary and Edward Watson took us in with open arms. Despite our condition and past, they still took care of us and give us all the help we needed. Every day, our mom would leave during work hours to take us to doctor's appointments just to make sure we were healthy and safe. Our foster parents would go out of their way to take us to various places like the park, the mall, stores, and the movies just to make sure we were happy.

They went above and beyond to make sure we got the right medication for all the issues we had putting us on focalin to help us with our issue. I remember my first day walking into their home it was unbelievable. I would ask questions live crazy knowing I finally get my own room to sleep in and get a real plate of food.

Seeing how life was changing in that moment made me probably on of the most happies kids on earth. Being able to get new clothes, shoes, and getting loved and cared for was one of the biggest moments in my siblings and I life. At that time my brother was born with a speaking disability, My younger sister was only 7 months old and needed a lot of care, and my older sister had gone through the process of getting glasses.

Figure 3: *"Captured in this moment: my siblings and I, gathered together, sharing laughter and warmth."*

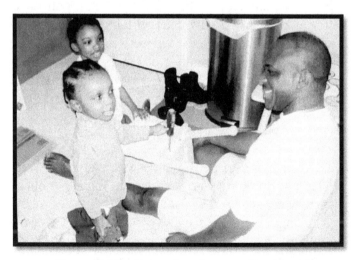

Figure 4: *"Crafting a chair for our table alongside my adopted father, each strike echoing our shared determination and bond.*

11

Even though they didn't have to, they went above and beyond to demonstrate their care for us, treating us as if we were their own children. They warmly welcomed us into the family, ensuring we felt included and loved. Our sister Necia, who was our adopted mom's daughter, took special care to organize little events for us to attend, and she even took the time to teach us basic hygiene skills, like how to take a proper bath and understand the importance of personal cleanliness.

Every year on August 12, since my birthday is the same day as their anniversary, they would dress us up and take us to a buffet or a restaurant to have a little party. After a few years, we discovered that our birth mom had a baby while in jail. Since we were a handful, it was first decided that we wouldn't take her in but since her foster parents wouldn't allow us to see her, our parents decided that she would live with us. At the age of 3, we were introduced to the church where everyone welcomed us with open arms. Although, at first, I never really liked it because it was something I never understood. Eventually, the atmosphere and happiness everyone showed made it something to enjoy.

Having to get up early to travel from Long Island to Brooklyn wasn't that much fun either but as time went on, we got used to it. Then after a few years, our bishop passed away and Mary, my adopted mother, was ordained as a pastor, and we started our own church.

The transition was difficult at first due to moving from an actual building to our living room.

It was new, having to move things around so everyone can fit, but God had a plan for us. As time went by, our numbers grew and we were able to move from our living room to our own building, which is under construction.

My educational journey began at Sunshine Learning Center in Queens, where I thrived in a supportive environment.

With caring educators and a nurturing family, I not only learned essential social skills but also gained independence. Through fun activities and engaging lessons, I discovered the joy of learning and prepared for future endeavors.

Luckily, my aunt, who was part of my adopted family, held the position of head of the school. This meant that I didn't have to mingle with unfamiliar faces.

Additionally, I found myself in the fortunate position of being taught by relatives, further ensuring that I was enveloped by the comforting presence of familiar individuals. This support network provided a sense of security and belonging during a period of significant adjustment and change in my life.

Being a part of Little Flower we had to meet with our parents every Friday as way to connect with them and for them to know and see that we are being taken care of and to make sure we were being feed well.

Every week became a new route for us from going to school, appointments, church, and then meet with our parents. Life was going great. We would go to place we didn't even know existed at the time.

Our parents did try was to get our adopted family in trouble because they wanted us back. But I just thank God that they didn't because going back to the way things were would be crushing mentally and physically.

Figure 5: *"Sharing a special bond at church for the first time with our adopted family."*

Figure 6: "Gathering around our beloved adopted mother, our smiles radiant with the warmth of her love, capturing a moment of cherished togetherness and gratitude."

Chapter 4

I remember my first day of elementary school, meeting new people and wanting to make new friends. I was so scared because the school was nothing like sunshine; there were way more kids, older and bigger.

I still wore a uniform at that time since my adopted family was used to the uniform as it was the way they dressed back in Jamaica. So, they did the same for us.

At the time, my older sister and I thought wearing it was fine, but all the other students in our classes thought otherwise. They made jokes about us and really didn't make us feel like we belonged there at that school, which really made things hard for us because as a kid my age, you want to make new friends and meet new people but having no one that cared was a lot on us. As time goes on, my older sister was able to get her way around with the people around her but sadly I wasn't able too.

As time went on, my older sister was able to get her way around with the people around her, but sadly I couldn't. In that time, due to everyone making fun of me, it caused me to not do well in class, ending up having to repeat the 3rd grade.

Everything together in that moment just didn't make anything easy for me. To know that I was trying so hard to please people to make friends and failing the 3rd grade just pushed me to being and quiet person.

I was too scared to tell my family because it wasn't like I knew any of the students so who would I be complaining about and it's hard to punish a whole class grade for picking on one student.

So going back for my second year in 3rd grade, I just shut myself away from everyone, hiding myself from everyone at school so that I don't get picked by anyone. Although I thought it would work at first, it really didn't change the outcome of the situation because now all the kids that were under me now know I failed the grade.

Since I was the only one that would wear uniform. I was constantly made fun of for the same thing as before and then even more things they thought was wrong with me. I realized that the more I stayed away from better I was able to do in classes, so I decided to continue what was doing.

Till one day one kids decided to come over my lunch table and sit with me and from that day we made a bond. Those few kids became my only friends in school.

As time went on our visits to our parents changed from one day at the agency to 2 days where one day we would meet our parents on Fridays at the agency then on Saturdays we would go to their house where we were dropped off the was picked up later back in the afternoon.

On my 12th birthday, as we were going to see my mom and dad, we saw our dad run out of the house and we knew something was wrong. So, we rushed up the stairs to see what happened. When we got to the house, my dad(adopted) made us sit in the living room while he tried to open the room my mom(birth) was stuck in.

As it turns out my dad was run away due to what he had did to our mom and didn't want to get arrested by the police.

After he left us we found out that our dad went to jail and went to court and signed a document saying that he has no legal responsibility for me my older sister and my younger siblings. At that time, it really hurt to know that our father would leave us no explanation and no reason as to why he did what he did to our mom.

Thankfully, we got there when we did because if we had gotten there any later, our mom could have possibly died. Even though we helped her on that day, four years later, we lost our real mom and then we went to court to finally finish the paperwork for the adoption. Since then, my adopted family has been a support factor for us.

As I start middle decided to make a fresh new start. Since I'm going into a new school I would try to open more to the people around me all though the bullying didn't stop I decided I wouldn't let it bother me.

Since I had my friends and adopted family always by my side to help guide me and give me help when needed. I put my best foot forward and doing the best I can.

Growing up, I never knew about any older siblings until I turned 12. My childhood was just like any other kid's, living each day without any knowledge of a larger family. The concept of being separated from siblings was alien to me; I believed there were only five of us.

A lot has changed for my siblings and I during that time. After our father gave away his rights, our mom was left to do things on her own. After a few months of visiting her she decided on moving to a place that was smaller and easier to clean and a place closer to the police station if ever needed.

In that time, she had just found out she had lung cancer and wasn't going to live long because she could afford to live get the treatment she needed to cure the cancer or to even decrease. It was sad to that every time we saw her she looked weaker than she was before.

That every time we meet our grandmother wanted to take us away which caused our mom to worry everyday which made her condition way harder on her than it was before. But After a year of fighting with the pain and sickness it caused she passed away at the age of 40.

Before she passed away she sign the adoption papers so that we can be adopted by the Watson family. For her funeral we traveled to Chicago to have her funeral and cremation and that was when we meet our real family face to face for the first time ever.

In my seventh-grade year was when we started the adoption process it wasn't something I was ready to tell people yet because there was a lot happening at that time and I just didn't want people in my business even though many people made jokes about the name change. But I didn't care because I know that I'm in a family that truly cares about my siblings and I, and that was all I needed.

But in the end, growing up in foster care was a transformative experience for me. Transitioning from a cramped one-bedroom apartment to a stable environment provided by my foster parents was a relief.

Their unwavering support and dedication helped ease the challenges of adapting to a new life. Despite the uncertainties of my early years, the nurturing environment provided by my foster family allowed me to flourish and find stability.

Throughout my upbringing, my foster parents played a pivotal role in shaping my life. Their unconditional love and tireless efforts to ensure our well-being fostered a strong bond between us.

From accompanying us to doctor's appointments to organizing family outings, their commitment to our happiness and growth was evident. Their kindness and generosity transformed our lives and instilled in us a sense of belonging and security.

Despite the challenges I faced in school, including bullying and academic setbacks, I remained determined to succeed. My experiences taught me the importance of resilience and perseverance in overcoming adversity.

With the support of my foster family and counselors, I navigated through difficult times and emerged stronger than before. Their guidance and encouragement fueled my drive to pursue my goals and strive for a better future.

Reflecting on my journey, I realize that my past does not define me. Despite the hardships I endured, I am grateful for the opportunities that have shaped me into the person I am today.

I am inspired to embrace life's challenges with courage and resilience, knowing that with determination and support, I can overcome any obstacle. My experiences have taught me that hope and perseverance are powerful catalysts for transformation, and I am committed to forging my path with resilience and optimism.

Now, I realize that there is always an opportunity to become anything you possibly want, no matter how bad your situation is. You can do anything you want in life; you just must have the desire and urge to do it. At the end of the day, even if you live with one parent or both or even none, whatever happened in your past will never define you.

Figure 7: *In the fun of Youth Service, we sang and prayed together, feeling happy and close.*

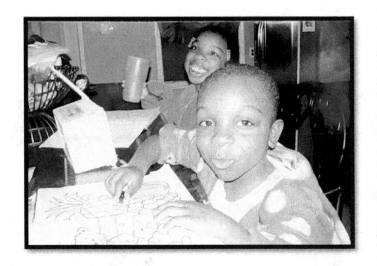

Figure 8: Coloring with my big sis: laughter, love, and colorful creations.

Figure 9: Playing in the snow

24

Figure 10: Having fun after church

Figure 11: Savoring a meal at Applebee's with my cherished adopted family, hearts full of love and laughter.

Figure 12: I'm all smiles, happily chilling out.

Figure 13: Graduating sunshine

Figure 14: "Children's Choir at Church".

Figure 15: "Youth Fellowship with Pastor and Elder"

Work Cited

"2003 Invasion of Iraq." Victory in War: Foundations of Modern Military Policy,
> by William C. Martel, Cambridge University Press, Cambridge, 2006, pp. 243–264.

Earle, C. Paul. "History Of Jamaica." Jamaican Embassy,
> https://www.embassyofjamaica.org/about_ja maica/history.htm#:~:text=The%20word%2 0Jamaica%20actually%20derives,Land%20 of%20wood%20and%20water%E2%80%9 D.&text=Christopher%20Columbus%20was %20the%20first,voyage%20to%20the%20N ew%20World

"Headlines for August 12, 2003." Democracy Now!.
> https://www.democracynow.org/2003/8/12/h eadlines.

Morrow, Kylie. "17 Amazing Things Jamaica Is Known for Beaches." Here Comes the Sun — The Official Beaches Resorts Travel & Lifestyle Blog, Here Comes The Sun —
> The Official Beaches Resorts Travel & Lifestyle Blog, 6 Oct. 2022, https://www.beaches.com/blog/things-jamaica-is-known-for/#:~:text=facts%20about%20Jamaica-,What%20is%20Jamaica%20known%20for %3F,inclusive%20resorts%20and%20majest ic%20waterfalls

U.S. Department of State, U.S. Department of State, https://history.state.gov/countries/jamaica#:~:text=Jamaica%20became%20independent%20on%20August,the%20American%20Embassy%20at%20Kingston.